ONE QUIET AFTERNOON

written by
Marc Gave

illustrated by
Scott Scheidly

HARCOURT BRACE & COMPANY

Orlando Atlanta Austin Boston San Francisco Chicago Dallas New York
Toronto London

I came home from school one day.
My mom had gone away.
A big baboon
Was up in my room
Picking out games to play.

3

I said, "Don't touch, you ape!"
He made a fast escape.
But his twin came in
With a silly grin
And went swinging from the drape,
the drape, the drape, the drape.

4

I hurried down the stairs,
And sitting in our chairs
Sat two huge dogs,
A couple of hogs,
And a pair of dancing bears.

A band began to play.
The animals started to sway.
The bears saw a chance
To try a new dance.
The parrot squawked, "Hooray!
Hooray! Hooray! Hooray!"

A horse carried in a cake.
She neighed, "I love to bake!"
But a hog lost control,
And swallowed it whole...
She got a stomachache.

I wondered what Mom would say
If she saw the animals play.
But they packed it all in
And went for a spin.
I hope they come back someday,
someday, someday, someday!